Nashua Public Library

34517011057100

DISCARDED

2009

J

Enjoy This Book!

Manage your library account and explore
all we offer by visiting us online at
www.nashualibrary.org.

Please return this on time, so
others can enjoy it, too.

If you are pleased with all that the
library offers, tell others.

@ **Nashua Public Library**
2 Court Street, Nashua, NM 03060
603-589-4600, www.nashualibrary.org

GAYLORD

D1306974

NASHUA PUBLIC LIBRARY

FIRST SCIENCE

Density

by Kay Manolis

Consultant:
Duane Quam, M.S. Physics
Chair, Minnesota State
Academic Science Standards
Writing Committee

BLASTOFF!
4
READERS

BELLWETHER MEDIA · MINNEAPOLIS, MN

JUV
531.14
MAN
NPL
1-3

Note to Librarians, Teachers, and Parents:

Blastoff! Readers are carefully developed by literacy experts and combine standards-based content with developmentally appropriate text.

Level 1 provides the most support through repetition of high-frequency words, light text, predictable sentence patterns, and strong visual support.

Level 2 offers early readers a bit more challenge through varied simple sentences, increased text load, and less repetition of high-frequency words.

Level 3 advances early-fluent readers toward fluency through increased text and concept load, less reliance on visuals, longer sentences, and more literary language.

Level 4 builds reading stamina by providing more text per page, increased use of punctuation, greater variation in sentence patterns, and increasingly challenging vocabulary.

Level 5 encourages children to move from "learning to read" to "reading to learn" by providing even more text, varied writing styles, and less familiar topics.

Whichever book is right for your reader, Blastoff! Readers are the perfect books to build confidence and encourage a love of reading that will last a lifetime!

This edition first published in 2009 by Bellwether Media.

No part of this publication may be reproduced in whole or in part without written permission of the publisher. For information regarding permission, write to Bellwether Media Inc., Attention: Permissions Department, Post Office Box 19349, Minneapolis, MN 55419.

Library of Congress Cataloging-in-Publication Data
Manolis, Kay.
  Density / by Kay Manolis.
    p. cm. – (Blastoff! readers. first science)
  Includes bibliographical references and index.
  Summary: "Simple text and full color photographs introduce beginning readers to density . Developed by literacy experts for students in kindergarten through third grade"—Provided by publisher.
    ISBN-13: 978-1-60014-224-6 (hardcover : alk. paper)
    ISBN-10: 1-60014-224-9 (hardcover : alk. paper)
    1. Specific gravity—Juvenile literature. 2. Water—Density—Juvenile literature. 3. Atmospheric density—Juvenile literature. I. Title.
  QC111.M36 2009
  531'.14–dc22   2008021302

Text copyright © 2009 by Bellwether Media Inc. BLASTOFF! READERS, and associated logos are trademarks and/or registered trademarks of Bellwether Media Inc.

SCHOLASTIC, CHILDREN'S PRESS, and associated logos are trademarks and/or registered trademarks of Scholastic Inc. Printed in the United States of America.

Contents

What Is Density?

Only two fish live in this tank.

Many more fish live in this tank. This tank has a much higher density of fish than the first tank. Density is a measure of the amount of objects in a certain space.

Density can tell you how crowded
an area is. Many people live close
together in this neighborhood. It has
high **population density**.

Fewer people live in this area. This area has much lower population density.

Density can also help describe a single object. It tells how much material an object contains, compared with the amount of space the object takes up.

Everything in the world is made of extremely tiny parts called **molecules**. These are clumps of even smaller pieces called **atoms**. Millions of molecules could fit on the tip of a pencil. **Solid** things, such as people and toys, are made of molecules. **Liquids**, such as water, are also made of them. Even **gases**, such as air, are made of molecules.

Molecules are arranged differently in solids, liquids, and gases. Molecules inside solid materials are crowded together. Many molecules fill a small area. Materials that have many molecules in a small area have high densities.

fun fact

Submarines have tanks that fill with either air or water. When the tanks fill with air, the whole submarine has a lower density than water, so it floats. When the tanks fill with water, the submarine's density is higher than water, so it sinks.

Molecules in liquids usually have more space around them. Compared to solids, there are fewer molecules in the same area. Gas molecules have even more space around them. There are even fewer molecules in the same area. Gases have low densities.

Imagine two objects that are about the same size but have different densities. The object with more density will **weigh** more. For example, this brick is made of clay, which is very dense.

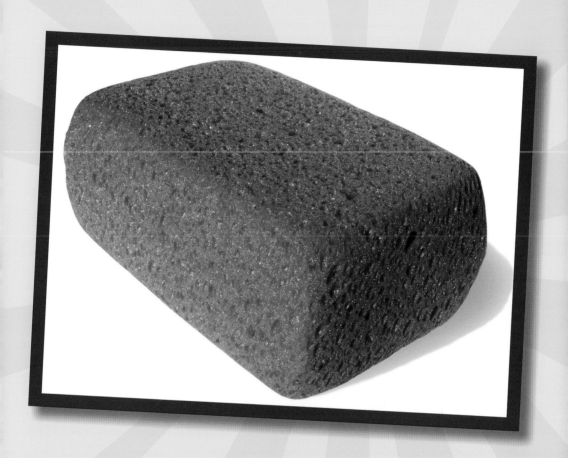

This sponge is much less dense than clay. The two objects take up about the same amount of space but the brick weighs a lot more.

Density in Water

A marble sinks in water. A beach ball floats. An object's density determines whether it will sink or float.

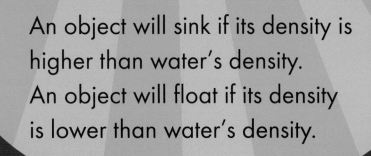

An object will sink if its density is higher than water's density. An object will float if its density is lower than water's density.

fun fact

Many ships are made of steel. Ordinarily, steel sinks in water. The shape of a ship holds a lot of air. This lets heavy steel float!

Water behaves differently than other materials. Most objects become more dense when they change from a liquid to a solid.

When water freezes into ice, its molecules move further apart. This means ice is less dense than water. That is why ice floats in water. Even huge **icebergs** float in water!

! fun fact

The density of ice is only slightly lower than that of water. For that reason ice floats "low" on the surface of water. This means that most of an iceberg floats below the surface.

Density in Air

Objects rise in air if their density is lower than the density of air. For example, these balloons are filled with a gas called **helium**. Helium's density is lower than air's density.

These balloons were filled by someone's breath. Human breath has density that is higher than air's density. These balloons sink to the floor.

NASHUA PUBLIC LIBRARY

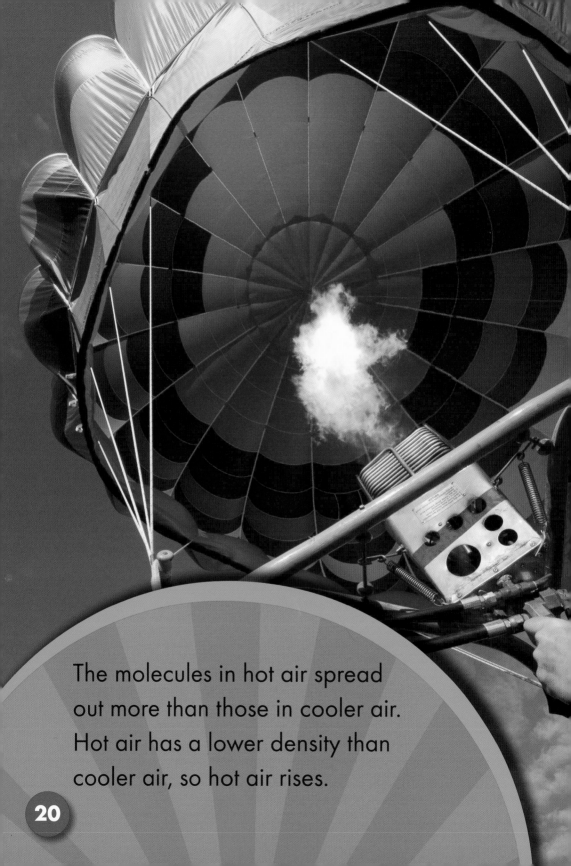

The molecules in hot air spread out more than those in cooler air. Hot air has a lower density than cooler air, so hot air rises.

A hot air balloon works because of density.
A burner heats air and lowers its density.
The hot air rises and lifts the balloon.
When the air cools or some hot air is let
out, the balloon comes down again.

Glossary

atoms—very tiny particles; atoms are the building blocks for everything in the world.

gas—a form of matter that has no definite shape or size

helium—a gas that is less dense than air

iceberg—a piece of ice that has broken off from a glacier or ice sheet and is floating in water

liquid—a form of matter that has no definite shape; a liquid can spill and flow.

molecules—the smallest parts of any material that have the properties of that material; molecules are groups of atoms.

population density—the number of people living in a certain area

solid—a form of matter that usually has a definite shape and size

weigh—to measure how heavy or light an object is; weight is a measure of the force of Earth's gravity on a living thing or object.

To Learn More

AT THE LIBRARY

Manolis, Kay. *Matter*. Minneapolis, Minn.: Bellwether, 2008.

Niz, Ellen Storm. *Floating and Sinking*. Minneapolis, Minn.: Capstone, 2006.

Walker, Sally M. *Matter*. Minneapolis, Minn.: Lerner, 2005.

ON THE WEB

Learning more about density is as easy as 1, 2, 3.

1. Go to www.factsurfer.com

2. Enter "density" into search box.

3. Click the "Surf" button and you will see a list of related web sites.

With factsurfer.com, finding more information is just a click away.

Index

The images in this book are reproduced through the courtesy of: ErickN, front cover; Juan Martinez, pp. 4, 5, 11 (left), 14, 20; Mitchell Funk / Getty Images, p. 6; Maremagnum / Getty Images, p. 7; Peter Beavis / Getty Images, pp. 8-9; Graeme Dawes, p. 10; Garry Gay / Alamy, p. 11 (right); Anke van Wyk, p. 12; Serghei Velusceac, p. 13; Ian D Walker, p. 15; Yva Momatiuk & John Eastcott / Getty Images, pp. 16-17; Kelvin Murray / Getty Images, p. 18; Bernd Opitz, p. 19; Elemental Imaging, p. 21.